A Tween Guide
to the
Science of God

By Jamie Head
Illustrated by Lisa Kosarich

Balboa Press books may be ordered through booksellers or by contacting:

Balboa Press
A Division of Hay House
1663 Liberty Drive
Bloomington, IN 47403
www.balboapress.com
1 (877) 407-4847

ISBN: 978-1-9822-0932-2 (sc)
ISBN: 978-1-9822-0931-5 (e)

Print information available on the last page.

Balboa Press rev. date: 08/03/2018

BALBOA®
PRESS
A DIVISION OF HAY HOUSE

CONTENTS

This book is dedicated to my beloved

Grandson, Grayson

PRINCIPLE:

A rule or law that never changes. It is the same for all people, everywhere, all the time...

Example: The Law of Gravity...

PRINCIPLE ONE:

God is Absolute Good, Everywhere Present

(God is ALL Good, ALL Love, and Exists Everywhere)

A few thousand years ago, the Old Testament was written. It is a combination of different stories written by different people over many years. These people were inspired to write about what and who they believed God to be at the time. Many of their writings are beautiful and show the respect of the people for a Higher Power in their lives.

The Old Testament was written before Jesus was born. The first 5 books, called the Torah, are the original Bible of the Hebrews (the Jewish people of Israel).

In those long-ago days, scientific facts were unknown. Natural disasters like hurricanes, volcanos and floods were assumed to be caused by an angry God for something the people had done wrong. When nature was cooperating and things were going well, the people believed that God was happy.

Even though **science** proves a very different God from the God of the Old Testament, most traditional Christian religions still believe in a God who has a temper, who passes out judgment, who favors some people over others, or even favors some religions over others. Of course, every religion is convinced that they are the **"true religion"**...

-There is only one religion though there are a hundred versions of it-

-G.B. Shaw

When we look at **science**, specifically the science called Quantum Physics (the science of Albert Einstein), it is believed that the Universe started with an event called the "Big Bang." Scientists believe that the Universe started from a speck of tremendous cosmic energy that exploded with so much force that the entire Universe was formed! Also, they agree, the Universe is still growing! According to the Quantum Physicists, there had to be a Creator that formed the energy that started this Cosmic Explosion...

The Creator is not a Being who is separate from us. The Creator is ALL THERE IS. God exists both **outside** and **everywhere** around us (called **transcendant**) and **inside** every cell and atom of ALL that exists (called **immanent**).

God is All the Energy that makes up everything in the Universe.

God is Principle...

Because God is ALL THERE IS, and because God is ALL LOVE and ALL GOOD, it is impossible for there to be a Devil or Satan. Satan would have to be a separate being; the opposite of God. But there cannot be an opposite to God because God is not a Being, God is ALL THERE IS, All the Energy that makes up the Universe...

Unfortunately, we all know there are people who do evil things. They don't understand that they are a part of God or that we are all connected. They feel fear, anger and isolation. Most people who choose to do what we consider evil acts, have been bullied or neglected. Sometimes being treated as if you don't exist is even worse than being picked on.

Sadly, these people don't realize how magnificent they are and don't know how to love themselves. Because they don't feel loved or worthy, they may strike out at others. They may say or do things that are mean or hurtful. We all know there are people who can act evil enough to harm or kill others.

But this is not the same as believing in Satan. Satan is the explanation that people from the Old Testament came up with to explain why some people acted in evil ways. "Evil" people were assumed to either worship Satan, or to have Satan inside them. Even people who had disabilities, mental illness, or seizures, were believed to have Satan inside them, or to have done something evil, or were born to parents who had done something evil. This is how the ancient people explained anything they didn't understand...

SATAN: "crazy thinking"

(definition in Aramaic, the language of Jesus)

Other names people use for GOD:

The Source

Universal Source

The Creator

Higher Power

Divine Mind

Divine Love

Life Force

Universal Intelligence

Creative Force

The Force (sound familiar?)

Just to name a few...

How do you feel about this kind of GOD?

PRINCIPLE TWO:

Human beings have a spark of divinity within them, the Christ Spirit within. Their essence is of God, and therefore they are also inherently Good.

(We humans have God flowing through us.
We are expressions of God in the World.
This is our Christ-Self, our Soul.)

Quantum Physics explains that the atoms that make up the molecules of our bodies can be traced to stars that have exploded into the galaxy. I guess we could say we are Children of the Stars. It also means that we humans are connected to animals, insects, birds, fish, plants, even rocks! Not only are we IN the Universe, but the Universe is IN us! We contain all the Life, Light and Energy of the Universe...

The definition of "Christ" in Hebrew is "Messiah."

MESSIAH means:

"Someone empowered by God to do Great Works in the World."

We each have a Christ-Self; the part of us known as the Soul. This is the part of us that is our expression of God in the World...

We can NEVER be separated from God. God lives and flows through each of us. When we act from our Christ-Self, we feel more of our connection with the Creative Force.

Being an indispensable (can't do without) part of the Universal Source is like being a piece of a puzzle. Each piece is totally unique. No piece can replace another piece. But they all connect to make a perfect and complete puzzle. The Universe would be incomplete if even one piece was missing...

The primary areas of Quantum Physics that appear to make up the Universe are Energy, Light and Vibration/Frequency. The PHOTON is one of the smallest units of energy in the Universe and is what makes up **light**. Energy produces all **light** and vibration that exists. The cells of our bodies use light to produce the energy they need to work properly. So, the sunlight we absorb is important to keep us healthy.

All living things also EMIT (give out) light and energy, including humans. The energy we give out is called our "Biofield." The light we emit is often called our "Aura." It is very unusual to see an aura but scientists can prove that the aura and biofield exist.

Some living organisms, especially sea animals, like jellyfish and a few other living organisms like fireflies, emit enough light that they are visible to our eyes. Often, in these animals, the emission of light is a way to communicate, protect themselves, or find food.

-In Each of us is a little of All of us –

-Lichtenberg

-With every breath inhaled, millions of atoms of air are exhaled somewhere else. You have Unity with everything you come in contact with –

-Unknown

(Meaning everything in the Universe is connected, even the air we breathe.)

-I have said, Ye are gods, and all of you are children of the Most High –

-Psalms 82:6 KJV

(Meaning You are One with God.)

-Everywhere you look in Science, it becomes harder to understand the Universe without God –

-Robert Herrman

-And God said Let there be light: and there was light –

-Genesis 1:3 KJV

-That was the true Light, which lighteth every man that cometh into the World –

-John 1:9 KJV

(Meaning the Universal Source is the True Light of the World that gives life to every human being.)

-God is a verb – an energy that moves through the Universe –

-Charles Holt

What do you think about the Energy of Light?

_____

_____

_____

_____

_____

_____

_____

_____

_____

_____

_____

_____

_____

_____

_____

_____

_____

_____

PRINCIPLE THREE:

Human beings create their experiences by the activity of their thinking. Everything in the manifest realm has its beginning in thought...

(The Law of the Universe is that when you think positive thoughts, positive things will happen in your life.)

THINK WISELY

The Law of Vibration states that NOTHING stands still. Everything in the Universe is moving (vibration) at different speeds (frequency). Even something that appears to stand still is vibrating, but at a different frequency than humans are able to experience. Think of it this way – the Earth spins at 1,038 miles an hour every day. We think we are standing still!

Our thoughts vibrate at certain frequencies which is why the thoughts and words we speak can be so powerful! They vibrate out into the Universe and are picked up like a cell phone or radio waves. Different thoughts also move at different frequencies. So, the frequency of the thoughts/words you put out will attract (draw to you) what you get back. Positive attracts positive. Negative attracts negative. This is known as the Law of Attraction.

Science has proven that our **thoughts** can affect the Universe. Scientists have actually been able to RECORD the amount of energy put out by thoughts!

We constantly make our world by our thoughts. Negative thoughts can only affect you if you let them. Keep your thoughts on what you WANT to happen in your life, not on what you don't want.

One way you can make a difference in the world is by the way you think. If everyone used the power of their thoughts to concentrate on Peace, on Love, on Caring for others, we could change the world! **Thoughts and Words** can be "catching"...

This gives us a whole new interpretation of the saying "Good Vibes"...

-For as a man thinketh in his heart, so is he -

-Proverbs 23:7 KJV

(Meaning the way a person thinks shows who he is.)

-All that we are is the result of what we have thought -

-The Buddha (approximately 400 years before the birth of Jesus)

-Our thoughts are the key which unlocks the doors of the Universe –

-S.M. Crothers

-If you think you can, or if you think you can't, either way you're right-

-Henry Ford

-Negative thoughts are the world's most communicable disease –

-Gene E. Clark

(Meaning be careful not to allow other people's negative attitudes influence your own.)

-If you want to find the secrets of the Universe, think in terms of Energy, Frequency, and Vibration -

-Nikola Tesla

-Everything is energy and that's all there is to it!
Match the frequency of the reality you want and you cannot help but get that reality.
This is not Philosophy.
This is Physics.-

-Albert Einstein

(Meaning if you concentrate on what you want in life, you will eventually get that life.)

-My mind is a garden,
My thoughts are the seeds,
My harvest will be either
Flowers or Weeds –

-Unknown

(Meaning how I think affects how positive or negative my attitude is.)

ABRACADABRA: "I create as I speak"
(definition in Aramaic, the language of Jesus)

Do you feel any differently about what you now think or say?

PRINCIPLE FOUR:

Prayer is creative thinking that heightens the connection with God-Mind and therefore brings forth wisdom, healing, prosperity and everything good ...

(Prayer is connecting your thinking with the Universal Source.)

Prayer is not something you do for God. Prayer is something you do for You. Prayer is what we do to connect in Oneness with ALL THERE IS. This connection gives our thoughts their power. Although, I am referring to Prayer here, the same connection can occur with Meditation (which is getting quiet, closing your eyes, and going inside your mind), or even watching the moon and stars, being in Nature, or doing anything that helps you feel peaceful and connected to the energy of the Universe.

As a young person, I used to wonder why the people of the Old Testament wrote about being "spoken to" by God. I always thought I was a good person who loved God, so why didn't God speak to me? In fact, I never hear of God speaking to anyone in the modern world. I was rather jealous of the people in ancient times who got to talk to God.

As an adult, I have learned that God does, indeed, communicate with us, just not in the way I expected. When I have a "gut-feeling" that I should go in a certain direction, I know the Source is guiding me. This is called INTUITION:

Knowing something without **physical proof**

When I am thinking of a friend I haven't seen in a long time and she calls me that same day, I know we are connecting through vibrations of the Universe. This is called COINCIDENCE or SYNCHRONICITY:

The unexpected occurrence of two events that happen at the **same time**...

Dreams, too, can be a way that God can communicate with us. As a young, soon-to-be mother, I was convinced that I was having a boy. My husband came from a family of all boys and it seemed likely that we would also have a boy. One night I had a vivid dream that I had a baby girl with red hair. Guess what? Yep, two months later I had a baby girl with RED hair!

When my daughter was twenty-six, she was diagnosed with cancer. While she was going through chemotherapy, she took my grandson shopping at a used bookstore. She found a book that she had been wanting to read and was pleased to find it there. When she got home and opened the book, there was a tiny note stuck inside. She was surprised and showed it to me. It said, handwritten, "It's not my time." I knew immediately that God was sending her a message. Most of our messages from God are through others, or through coincidence, as we know. I explained to her that this meant she was going to be okay. This was ten years ago and she is still doing well.

Principle Four: Quotes and Bible Passages

-Seek ye the Kingdom of God; and all these things shall be added unto you -

-Luke 12:31 KJV

(Meaning when you have a connection with the Source, you will discover that you will have everything else you need.)

-For your Father knoweth what things ye have need of, before ye ask -

-Matthew 6:8 KJV

(Meaning the Creator knows your thoughts.)

Have you ever had a dream that came true? A gut-feeling?

_____

_____

_____

_____

_____

_____

_____

_____

_____

_____

_____

_____

_____

_____

_____

_____

PRINCIPLE FIVE:

Knowing and understanding the Laws of Life, also called Truth, are not enough. A person must also live the Truth that he or she knows ...

(Understanding the Principles isn't enough. We should express our understanding by the way we live.)

It takes courage to be in a Human body! We live in a world full of emotions: frustration, sadness, competition, anxiety, and feeling unloved. It is important that we love and appreciate Ourselves. It is important that we understand that ALL people make mistakes, and see the good in everyone. Mistakes are a part of being human. They are a learning experience that will encourage us to do better next time. Mistakes and failure are NOT who we are! They are only a temporary setback that will ultimately move us forward in life...

Self-Love is the most important thing we can do for ourselves. This doesn't mean 'stuck up" or "better than you' behavior. Most people who act like that don't feel good about themselves and their way of trying to feel better is to try to make others look bad. It is important that we accept ourselves and everyone else as we are. We are all magnificent beings made from the Energy of the Universe and nothing anyone says or does will EVER change that!

I know of a man who was teased and bullied as a teen. He was overweight and felt bad about himself. Unfortunately, his family was not very supportive and he felt lonely and unloved. He was feeling so depressed that he considered killing himself. One day at school, a girl who knew him, invited him over to her house after school. When he got there, her mom had baked him a birthday cake. He had a wonderful time visiting and eating cake.

This one act of kindness caused him to rethink his life. He went back to school and decided to keep trying. This man is now married, with kids of his own. He has a successful career and is very happy. He feels that he owes his life to that one act of kindness.

You NEVER know how powerful an act of kindness can be!

-*We must be the change we wish to see in the world -*

-Mohandas Gandhi

-*Be Yourself, Everyone else is already taken -*

-Unknown

-*An apology is the superglue of Life – it can repair just about Everything -*

-Lynn Johnson

-*Mistakes are the portals of discovery -*

-James Joyce

(Meaning mistakes are a great learning experience if we are ready.)

-*A hero is a man who can change his fear into positive energy -*

-A.S. Neill

-*"Spirituality" is living the ordinary life in an extraordinary way -*

-Huston Smith

How do you feel about being an Expression of the Creator and having the power to make a difference in the World?

JESUS

We can't finish an explanation of God and the Principles without an understanding of who Jesus was ...

In most traditional Christian religions, Jesus is considered "The Only Son of God." His "destiny" was to die for "our sins," the mistakes of humanity. Jesus has been treated as a supernatural being – someone more God than human.

But, Jesus never said He was different from any of us. He was a Master Teacher who wanted to help us learn how to connect with the Creator the way He did. He wanted us to know that we are ALL born to be Expressions of God. He wanted us to understand that we ALL have the abilities He had. The only difference between Jesus and us is that Jesus lived from His Christ-Self ALL the time! He knew that we have the ability to do the same thing. He never expected to be worshipped. He never expected to have a religion named after Him. He considered Himself to be a faithful Jewish man who discovered a way to connect powerfully with the Universal Source.

The New Testament was written after Jesus died. Jesus never wrote down any of His teachings, so we have to rely on the Gospel writers ("Gospel" means the teachings of Jesus) to tell us about His life and teachings. They did the best they could, based on the stories passed down through the years. It is most likely that they added their own understanding of what they thought the stories meant. So, all we have is what the Bible and the Apocrypha (stories not included in the Bible) tell us.

Jesus: Quotes and Bible Passages

-Jesus answered them, Is it not written in your Law, I said, ye are gods? -

-John 10:34 KJV
(remember Psalms 82:6?)

-Verily, verily, I say unto you, he that believeth on me, the works that I do shall he do also; and greater works than these shall he do -

-John 14:12 KJV

(Meaning you can do all that Jesus did if you live from your Christ-Self.)

-Jesus knew that "I, of myself, can do nothing" but as long as He kept Himself Centered in God, He could do All things -

-Unknown

-YE ARE THE LIGHT OF THE WORLD. LET YOUR LIGHT SO SHINE BEFORE MEN -

-Matthew 5:14, 16 KJV

Any other feelings or thoughts?

INSPIRATION FROM:

Connie Fillmore Bazzy: Originator of the concept of the Five Principles of Unity

Eric Butterworth: *Celebrate Yourself*
The Quest for Unity
Discover the Power Within You

Mary Manin Morrissey: *No Less than Greatness*

Ellen Debenport: *The Five Principles*

The Film: "What the Bleep Do We Know?"

Exhibit: "Creatures of Light" featured at the Denver Museum of Nature and Science – June 2018

Illustrated by: Lisa Kosarich

Printed in the United States
By Bookmasters